IT'S TIME TO LEARN ABOUT ALLIGATORS

It's Time to Learn about Alligators

Walter the Educator

Silent King Books
A WhichHead Entertainment Imprint

Copyright © 2025 by Walter the Educator

All rights reserved. No part of this book may be reproduced in any manner whatsoever without written per- mission except in the case of brief quotations embodied in critical articles and reviews.

First Printing, 2024

Disclaimer

This book is a literary work; the story is not about specific persons, locations, situations, and/or circumstances unless mentioned in a historical context. Any resemblance to real persons, locations, situations, and/or circumstances is coincidental. This book is for entertainment and informational purposes only. The author and publisher offer this information without warranties expressed or implied. No matter the grounds, neither the author nor the publisher will be accountable for any losses, injuries, or other damages caused by the reader's use of this book. The use of this book acknowledges an understanding and acceptance of this disclaimer.

It's Time to Learn about Alligators is a collectible early learning book by Walter the Educator suitable for all ages belonging to Walter the Educator's Time to Eat Book Series. Collect more books at WaltertheEducator.com

USE THE EXTRA SPACE TO TAKE NOTES AND DOCUMENT YOUR MEMORIES

ALLIGATORS

Down in the swamp where the waters flow,

It's Time to Learn about

Alligators

Lives a reptile you might know.

With scaly skin and teeth so white,

The alligator is quite a sight!

It has a tail so long and strong,

That swishes as it swims along.

With webbed feet, it glides with ease,

Through rivers, lakes, and swampy trees.

Its eyes peek out, just like a spy,

Watching birds and fish pass by.

It stays so still, but don't be fooled,

It moves so fast when it is schooled!

Its teeth are sharp, its bite is tight,

It holds on strong with all its might.

But don't you fear, don't run away,

It mostly hunts at night, not day.

It's Time to Learn about
Alligators

When it gets too hot and bright,

It digs a hole and hides from light.

A muddy pool, so cool and deep,

A perfect place to rest and sleep.

Alligator moms are great,

They guard their eggs and never wait.

They build a nest and watch with care,

Until their babies fill the air.

The little ones are small and sweet,

With tiny tails and snappy feet.

They chirp and call, they stay close by,

Until they're big enough to try.

Though strong and fierce, they have a plight,

As humans change their homes so bright.

They need the swamps, the lakes, and trees,

It's Time to Learn about
Alligators

To live their lives just as they please.

We must protect these ancient friends,

So their strong story never ends.

By keeping waters clean and pure,

We help their future stay secure.

So if you see one, big or small,

Just watch it swim, but don't get tall!

Respect its space and let it be,

It's Time to Learn about
Alligators

The mighty gator, wild and free!

ABOUT THE CREATOR

Walter the Educator is one of the pseudonyms for Walter Anderson. Formally educated in Chemistry, Business, and Education, he is an educator, an author, a diverse entrepreneur, and he is the son of a disabled war veteran. "Walter the Educator" shares his time between educating and creating. He holds interests and owns several creative projects that entertain, enlighten, enhance, and educate, hoping to inspire and motivate you. Follow, find new works, and stay up to date with Walter the Educator™

at WaltertheEducator.com

www.ingramcontent.com/pod-product-compliance
Lightning Source LLC
LaVergne TN
LVHW052016060526
838201LV00059B/4057